Over the past few years we have all come to realize that the use of social media has become an increasingly important element of any organizations' marketing, communications and community building work. Yet the democratic, transparent and public nature of social media means that staff and lay leaders of Jewish organizations recognize these shifts, and equip ourselves to use these tools strategically, intentionally, wisely and for good.

It is therefore our pleasure to present you with the *Social Media Policy Workbook for Jewish Organizations,* developed by social media experts Darim Online in partnership with Idealware.

This workbook is custom-built for Jewish organizations interested in using social media to its full potential. It is a resource for those looking for guidance to help them better understand, and make important decisions about how to integrate social media into your organization's work to achieve the best results, and avoid missteps.

The new technologies and cultural shifts around communicating messages, engaging and motivating stakeholders, reaching new audiences, creating content, and strengthening your brand can be overwhelming. At the same time, we believe such work is essential for Jewish organizations, day schools and camps to succeed in their important missions of creating a new generation of Jewish-ly literate and engaged young Jews.

We hope you will use this workbook as both a resource and an opportunity to gain fluency in this area, and to help you be proactive in thinking strategically about social media culture and policies in your work.

As always, we thank you for the meaningful work you are currently doing in communications, relationship-building, and advocacy around Jewish education.

Sincerely,

Deena Fuchs,
Director of Strategic Partnerships
The AVI CHAI Foundation

DARIM
ONLINE

TABLE OF CONTENTS

ABOUT THE AUTHORS

Darim Online

Lisa Colton is the founder and president of Darim Online, a nonprofit organization dedicated to helping Jewish organizations thrive in the connected age through effective social media and leadership strategies. Lisa works to empower staff and volunteer leaders to use social media and network strategies to advance their missions and achieve their goals. A graduate of Stanford University, Livnot U'lehibanot, and The Pardes Institute for Jewish Studies, she has received the Jewish Communal Service Association's Young Professional Award, The Nonprofit Technology Network's NTEN-Y Award, Hillel's Exemplar of Excellence Award, and most recently the National Jewish Outreach Partnership's Jewish Influencer Award. Lisa also serves on the boards of her children's school and The Local Food Hub in Charlottesville, Virginia where she lives with her husband, two kids, a dog named Stella, and a flock of backyard chickens.

Miriam Brosseau is the Associate Director for Network Initiatives in a joint position with Darim Online and The Jewish Education Project. In both capacities she works with individuals and groups to bridge the divide between online and on-land networks, encourage cooperation and collaboration, and help them to embody organizational values and vision in all their efforts. Miriam holds a BA in Jewish Studies and Modern Hebrew from the University of Wisconsin-Madison, and an MA in Jewish Professional Studies from Spertus Institute in Chicago, where she focused her learning on the intersection of new Jewish culture, educational vision, and the social web. Miriam is part of the ROI community of young Jewish innovators, and was named to the Jewish Week's "36 Under 36" list of change-makers in greater New York City in 2012. Miriam is half of the "biblegum pop" duo Stereo Sinai along with her husband, producer Alan Jay Sufrin. In her free time, Miriam can be found reading, roller skating, and dangling things in front of her cats.

Idealware

Andrea Berry oversees Idealware's fundraising and training activities, including live and online seminars, curriculum development, sponsorship, and corporate and individual giving. She is also Idealware's resident expert in social media tools and techniques.

Laura Quinn is Idealware's Executive Director, and as such, directs Idealware's research, writing, and training to provide candid reports and articles about nonprofit software. Prior to joining Idealware, Laura founded Alder Consulting, where she helped nonprofits create internet strategies, select appropriate software, and then build sophisticated websites on a limited budget.

Thank you to the following people whose invaluable assistance helped bring this Workbook to life: Caren Levine, Rabbi Danny Burkeman, Rabbi Adam Grossman, Rabbi Amy Bolton, Dru Greenwood, Rabbi Josh Yuter, Paul Wieder, Ira Wise, and Deborah Grayson Riegel.

HOW THIS WORKBOOK WAS FUNDED

Darim Online is thankful to many partners and supporters who have made this Workbook possible. Thank you to The Union for Reform Judaism (URJ), The AVI CHAI Foundation, and See3 Communications for sponsoring this Workbook. And thank you to UJA Federation of New York, and The Covenant Foundation that have both funded work that has led to this Workbook. We are thankful for their support, inspiration and commitment to advancing the Jewish community for success in the connected age.

Darim Online partnered with Idealware, a leader in nonprofit technology research, reporting, and training, to develop this Social Media Policy Workbook. Idealware and their funders supported their contributions to the Workbook, and Idealware is disseminating a non-Jewish version to the general nonprofit community. More information about the general nonprofit edition can be found at http://www.idealware.org.

idealware

INTRODUCTION

Some organizations jump into social media with great excitement. Others with great trepidation. What we know is that the rules of engagement in social media are in many ways fundamentally different than those of other communication tools we've used in the past: skills of staff and volunteers vary widely, employees may blend their personal and professional lives, and perhaps most importantly, the "audience" can talk back and to each other. The open and community-based aspects of social media can be a huge benefit for nonprofits looking to reach out to new audiences and engage their existing base. In this new landscape it's important for each organization to evaluate how they can and should be using these powerful tools.

As we've trained, coached, and consulted with hundreds of organizations from synagogues and day schools to federations and foundations, we've found that those leaders who are most nervous about social media are uncomfortable with the idea of losing control of their brand, message, and/or authority. In some organizations, the staff who are the most social media savvy (and thus a great asset to organizations wishing to move forward) may not be maximizing their potential because they don't yet know what's appropriate and encouraged.

A good social media policy provides clear guidelines as to how staff should represent themselves and the organization when posting and interacting with the community, freeing them up to think more strategically. A social media policy is also likely to help leadership feel more comfortable with the less formal nature of social media by letting them establish boundaries for its use. Often to gain comfort and confidence, we need to reduce the fear, get clear on expectations, and be on the same page with our staff, supervisors, board members, and the community.

This Workbook is designed to help you, as an organization, ask important questions about social media. In our experience, developing a social media policy as a team is a valuable process by which all parties can voice concerns, examine opportunities, develop a shared vocabulary, and together articulate the "rules of engagement" for your work. Chances are good that you'll find the conversations you have as a team are every bit as important as the product you end up with. Raising the right questions and exploring these issues can be a challenge, but it's a valuable step in the maturation of a modern organization.

Consider these worksheets to be conversation starters—and make sure you have the right voices in those conversations. Who should be involved? It depends on your organization, but examples include the people defining your overall communications strategy, those defining your social media goals and activities, those managing the actual social media channels on a day-to-day basis, someone from the executive team, and a board member. Developing a social media policy is also a great opportunity to invite social media savvy members of your community to share their expertise and engage them as future leaders of your community.

If you're a one-man-or-woman band tackling social media yourself, pat yourself on the back, and then pull in one or two people anyway to have multiple perspectives represented and to make sure the organization as a whole understands and buys into the decisions you're making.

There's no right or wrong way to draft a policy. Some organizations have 5 bullet points, others have 10 page documents. Some are very loose guidelines, while others are quite rigid, formal policies. Throughout the Workbook we've added vignettes from organizations which have created social media policies or guidelines to show some real-world examples of what's involved. We've also included sample language from policies and guidelines for inspiration, to help you see how some organizations have approached the issues you're discussing. By proceeding through this Workbook with your team, you'll find the approach that's right for you.

We are not lawyers; thus, we are not recommending any particular positions, decisions, or language. This Workbook is intended to facilitate your own internal process, and we recommend you include or consult a lawyer to advise on any legal details that apply to your work, such as HIPPA compliance for health care organizations.

Finally, embrace the process. The development of a social media policy can be as valuable as the document itself (if not more so). While collaboratively drafting your policy, you may uncover other ways for your organization to translate its values and best use its human resources to thrive in the connected age. And remember that this can—and should—be a living document. Technology changes, culture changes, and your organization's social media strategy will evolve too. Thus, make sure that your language isn't so rigid that it will be outdated in a year, and make plans to revisit your policy regularly and update it as the technologies (and your uses of them) mature.

When the Israelites entered into the Covenant at Mt. Sinai, they proclaimed: *na'aseh v'nishmah,* "We will do, and then we will understand" (Exodus 24:7). They affirmed that to truly understand a new way of approaching the world, they had to dive in and give it a try. So too with social media; greater understanding comes through thoughtfully and intentionally giving it a go!

So, are you ready? Gather your team together, start the Social Media Policy Workbook, and enjoy the journey...

CREATING THE TEAM

When the executive director of a mid-sized family service agency decided that an organization-wide review of policies and procedures would also be a good time to create a social media policy, staff jumped on the opportunity.

"The way we approached creating a policy was that I worked with the social media committee—myself, another staff member, and board members—and wrote most of the policy," said the program director. "I got feedback from them, and from the board and legal counsel to the agency. They made very important suggestions, and I think that's critical to get all that input."

Interested in learning from others who are working on their social media policy too? Join the discussion in the Social Media Policy Facebook group at http://www.facebook.com/groups/socialmediapolicy.

DARIM

1. WHAT DOES A SOCIAL MEDIA POLICY MEAN TO YOU?

"One should always be as flexible as a reed, and not be rigid as a cedar." Talmud, Taanit 20a.

Different organizations will start this Workbook from different places. Some have vast experience in social media, others have let an "accidental techie" advance their work, and others are yet to really get started. Thus, as we begin, we encourage you to explore what you want to get from this process. How does your organization need to mature to be successful in social media, and what does your team need to move forward with confidence?

Tactics or Vision?

First, think through how much guidance you want to give staff in your policy by plotting yourself on the spectrum below. Make a mark anywhere on the line:

Our policy should spell out pretty much everything staff should or should not do.

Our policy should provide tactics for important situations and guidelines to inform staff decisions.

Our policy is a vision and strategy document to help staff make their own decisions.

How would you define the purpose of your policy, based on your location on the spectrum? Use one of the definitions given above, or craft your own.

Legal or Informal?

A social media policy can be very informal or quite formal, depending on what you need it to achieve. Yours can be a general guideline, a *brit* (covenant) with your staff, volunteers, and/or community, or a formal legal document. How formal or informal do you want your policy to be? Do you typically have lawyers sign off on policy documents? Is there an internal sensitivity in regard to this particular policy? How legal in nature do you think your policy should be? Plot yourself on the line.

The lawyers are going to need to be involved in this process.

We will need a lawyer to sign off on it, but we want to write it in a friendly and approachable way.

It should provide guidance and education when it comes to legally sensitive issues, but it doesn't need to be legally binding.

It will be a *brit* (covenant) between parties involved in our social media use, establishing expectations and norms without being a formal policy.

We want to provide informal guidelines to staff and community members.

How would you define the necessity of including a lawyer in your process, based on your location on the spectrum? Use one of the definitions given above, or craft your own.

DARIM
ONLINE

How Widely Will You Distribute It?

Who is this policy for? A few key staff, certain staff, all staff? How about volunteers who hold formal (e.g. a board member) or informal (e.g. helping out with an event) roles? What about the user community who interacts in your online spaces?

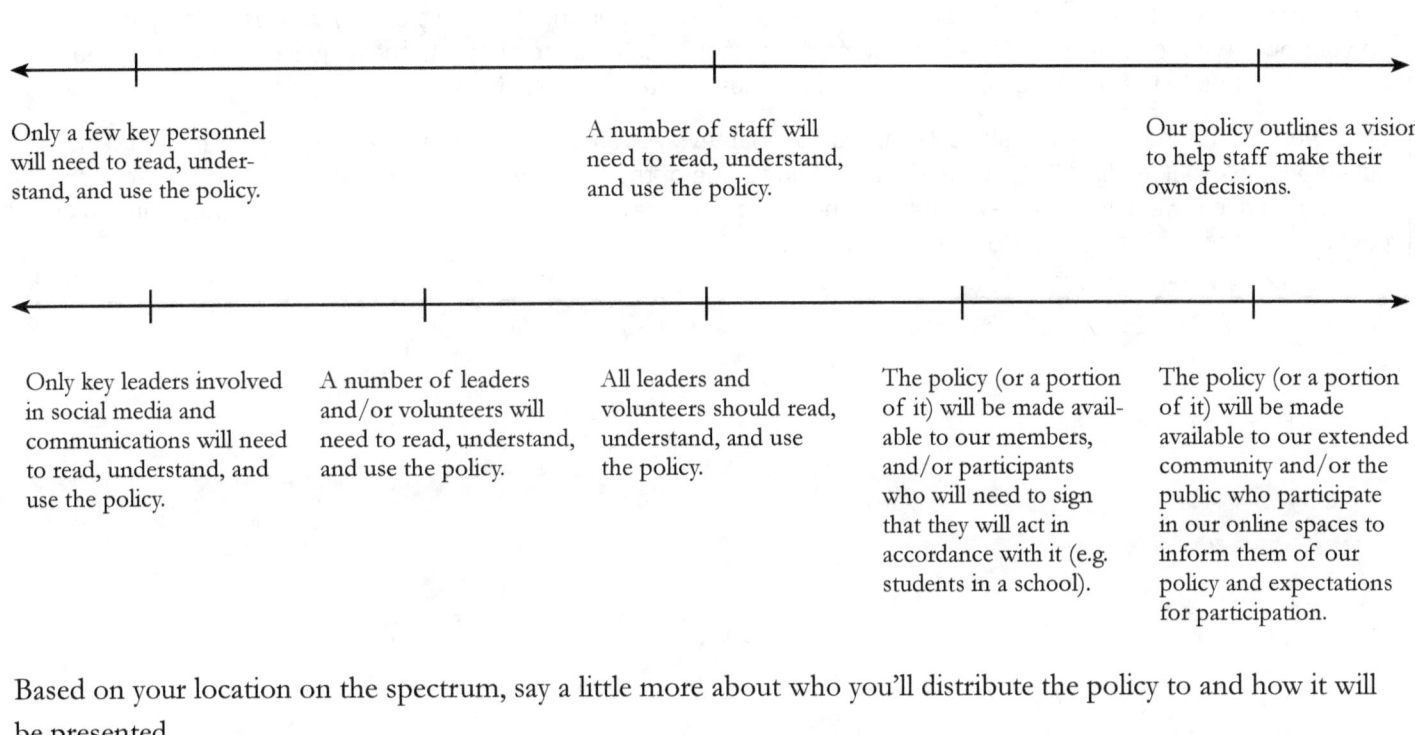

Only a few key personnel will need to read, understand, and use the policy.

A number of staff will need to read, understand, and use the policy.

Our policy outlines a vision to help staff make their own decisions.

Only key leaders involved in social media and communications will need to read, understand, and use the policy.

A number of leaders and/or volunteers will need to read, understand, and use the policy.

All leaders and volunteers should read, understand, and use the policy.

The policy (or a portion of it) will be made available to our members, and/or participants who will need to sign that they will act in accordance with it (e.g. students in a school).

The policy (or a portion of it) will be made available to our extended community and/or the public who participate in our online spaces to inform them of our policy and expectations for participation.

Based on your location on the spectrum, say a little more about who you'll distribute the policy to and how it will be presented.

_____

_____

Is it Part of Something Else?

Will the policy be part of another document, like an employee handbook, or does it need to be in the same style as another document? Do existing policies already include information about this issue? How to these other policies influence how you will create a social media policy?

_____

_____

_____

DARIM
ONLINE

SHOULD THE LAWYERS BE INVOLVED?

A large family foundation has specific concerns about crossing the line into lobbying and jeopardizing their 501(c)(3) status. Because foundation leadership is unwilling to test the waters around these legal issues, current practice is to avoid such topics entirely.

"We're very conservative about that," said the Director of Communications. "If the legal line is somewhere around *here*, we're 15 miles in the other direction, just to be safe." The law in this area is so gray, you have to interpret it on your own. What does it mean to retweet something? Is that an endorsement? All these questions where the law hasn't caught up to the technology, each organization has to interpret it for itself.

She's worried that having to run all posts through a legal review would degrade the organization's ability to take advantage of social media. "We'd run the risk of losing some of the 'socialness' and the immediacy that makes social media effective if we have to run everything through legal before we post it," she said. To that end, she's cautious to post only things clearly distinct from politics, which is limiting.

Develop a Plan for Your Organization

Summarize your position on this topic (the language you use here can be the basis for your policy document).

_____

_____

_____

_____

_____

What other information do you need to gather?

_____

_____

_____

_____

What other questions has this brought up that you need to address?

_____

_____

_____

_____

2. YOUR ORGANIZATION'S VALUES IN SOCIAL MEDIA

"The Jewish people are recognized by three qualities: They are compassionate, they are modest, and they perform acts of loving kindness." Talmud, Y'vamot 79a.

Engaging in social media is your organization's opportunity to genuinely reflect online who you are on-land. As such, your social media policy should not live in a vacuum, but should be guided by the values and vision of your organization. Use this worksheet to reflect on your organization's values and think about how to translate those values into guidelines for social media.

Your Mission and Vision

What is the mission of your organization? What kind of impact is your organization working to achieve? How are you trying to influence your community? Write your organization's mission and vision statements below for reference.

_____

_____

_____

_____

_____

_____

_____

Your Values

Though technology is constantly changing, foundational values endure. What values define your organization? What core concepts do you strive to embody? Define a list of about six core values—be they Jewish, professional, or universal—which are central to your organization's work. Feel free to use the lists on the next page for inspiration.

1. _____   4. _____

2. _____   5. _____

3. _____   6. _____

DARIM
ONLINE

POSSIBLE ORGANIZATIONAL VALUES		POSSIBLE JEWISH ORGANIZATIONAL VALUES
Altruism	Fun	Beauty (*Yofi/Hiddur Mitzvah*)
Agility	Honesty	Compassion (*Rachamim*)
Approachability	Impartiality	Honoring Creation (*Kavod Habriyot*)
Attentiveness	Ingenuity	Jewish Peoplehood (*Klal Yisrael*)
Caring	Innovation	Mutual Responsibility (*Areyvut*)
Community Focus	Modesty	Proper Behavior (*Derekh Eretz*)
Collaboration	Peacefulness	Publicizing a Miracle (*Pirsumei Nisah*)
Craftsmanship	Polish	Pursuing Peace (*Rodef Shalom*)
Creativity	Passion	Repairing the World (*Tikkun Olam*)
Devoutness	Realism	Returning/Repentance (*Teshuvah*)
Diversity	Responsiveness	Righteousness/Charity (*Tzedaka*)
Economy	Safety	Thankfulness (*Hoda'ah*)
Expertise	Science	Welcoming Guests (*Hachnasat Orchim*)
Fairness	Solidarity	
Friendliness	Sustainability	

For additional Jewish values to consider, see: http://www.morim.org/getfile.aspx?id=4924

For a crowd-sourced list of Jewish values associated with social media, see:
http://www.darimonline.org/blog/jewish-values-and-social-media-meta-converastion

How Do Your Values Apply to Social Media?

Some of these values will translate almost directly to social media guidelines, while others may be less useful. Consider how you might translate them below.

	VALUE	WHAT DOES THIS MEAN FOR YOUR PRESENCE IN THE SOCIAL MEDIA WORLD?
	ex. Generosity (*Nedivut*)	We will proactively provide support and resources to our community through social media, listening to their needs, and giving before receiving.
	ex. Responsiveness	We will focus on listening to what others are saying in our community and make a priority to respond in a quick and informative manner.
	ex. Impartiality	We will not take a stance on political issues in our posts, nor offer recommendations not grounded in facts.
1.		
2.		
3.		
4.		
5.		
6.		

CREATING A POLICY TO REFLECT THE ORGANIZATION'S VALUES

The team that created the social media policy for a Jewish agency all agreed they did not want the policy to be a list of "do nots," but a living document that reflected the nonprofit's goals and values.

"We started 'meta' and got to the 'macro,'" said the program director. "We started with the Jewish values particular to us, but any organization has a mission and core values. One example for us was a Hebrew term that translates loosely to 'promoting unity into the community,' (*K'lal Yisrael*) which we see as 'to promote community dialogue.' Part of that was enhancing community partnership on social media."

Develop a Plan for Your Organization

Summarize your position on this topic (The language you use here can be the basis for your policy document).

_____

_____

_____

_____

_____

What other information do you need to gather?

_____

_____

_____

_____

_____

What other questions has this brought up that you need to address?

_____

_____

_____

_____

_____

DARIM
ONLINE

3. SOCIAL MEDIA ROLES: WHO DOES WHAT?

"But Moses' father-in-law said to him, "'The thing you are doing is not right; you will surely wear your-self out, and these people as well. For the task is too heavy for you; you cannot do it alone. Now listen to me. I will give you counsel, and God be with you! You represent the people before God: you bring the disputes before God, and enjoin upon them the laws and the teachings, and make known to them the way they are to go and the practices they are to follow."' Exodus 18:17-20.

Determining who's in charge of your social media activities is essential to assigning responsibility and accountability throughout your organization for the channels you use. When clear roles are defined, your organization can more easily execute strategy and understand who can–and who cannot–do what. If you work in a small organization, this might be a simple worksheet, but it's still worth defining the roles.

You may notice as you move through these discussions that your best social media skills reside with people who have unrelated (or moderately related) job descriptions. We often call these folks the "acci-dental techies"–the people who have taken initiative and responsibility for an organization's technology infrastructure, even though their professional training and/or job description does not include tasks of this kind. You may come to appreciate what they've already been doing, and start to think about the optimal staffing structure to achieve your goals in the connected age.

Who's in Charge? Who's in charge of all social media and social media strategy for your organization?

_____

Who oversees your communications calendar and coordinates between channels? (This may be the same person as above.)

_____

If someone has a question as to what content is appropriate or how to handle a sticky situation, with whom should they speak?

_____

If someone has a question about launching a new online space or organization-related account, with whom should they speak?

_____

If someone has a technical question or needs assistance to execute a task, with whom should they speak?

_____

Different Roles for Different Channels

Next, list in the left-hand column each individual/job title with a role in your social media activities. For each channel:

1. Identify the lead staff member in charge of the channel. Mark the box with a star.

2. For anyone else who is EXPECTED to post on the channel, mark the box with a E.

3. For anyone else who is ALLOWED to post on the channel, mark the box with an A.

4. For any other content contributor who funnels content to one of the people identified above, mark the box with a CC.

PERSON/ ROLE	FACEBOOK	TWITTER	YOUTUBE	BLOG	CONTENT CURATION (e.g. Pinterest, Delicious)	LOCATION BASED SER- VICES (e.g. Foursquare, facebook places)	OTHER
George	E	*		A			
Linda	*	E		CC			
Sarah	A		*	*			

DARIM

4. WHAT SHOULD YOU SAY ONLINE?

"Avtalyon would say: Scholars, be careful with your words..." Pirkei Avot 1:13.

What should your staff be posting and sharing online? What topics should they never post about? Think through your own guidelines.

Look back at the core values you wrote in Worksheet #2. If staff were to ask themselves three questions before each post they make online, what three questions would best ensure that their posts fit in with your core values?

1. _____

2. _____

3. _____

EXAMPLE

A Jewish Day School is interested in engaging the parents of their current students through social media. They would like to do more than share pictures of Purim parties and Torah study sessions. The staff regularly engages in discussions around new educational models and theories, incorporating what they can into their teaching as it fits with the philosophy of the school. They are thought leaders in education, and model this online by posting links to the articles they are discussing as a staff on their Facebook page every week with insightful questions to promote discussion. Before they post an article, they ask themselves the following questions: 1. How can we include the perspective of the school in the phrasing of the question, post, or follow-up? 2. Imagine a prospective family seeing this piece on Facebook—what value will this content add for them, and what message will it send to them about our school?

Charlene Li, in her book <u>Open Leadership,</u> describes transparency as a sandbox—the space in which you can be most open and flexible. There are parameters; the sandbox may be large or small, or change in size, but it is not without definition. For instance, it may be permissible, and even useful, for a synagogue to share the data from a recent congregational survey about their programs (that kind of transparency could help the congregation foster dialogue and improve their engagement efforts). On the other hand, it is unwise to share publicly the salary information of the staff; that may be considered moving beyond the space of the sandbox. Ultimately, though, creating that space and welcoming your community into it helps breed trust. Use the following 3 questions to articulate the inside, the outside, and the boundaries of your sandbox. What topics or types of information are okay to share transparently on social media?

1. _____

2. _____

3. _____

DARIM
ONLINE

What topics or types of information, if any, require approval prior to posting?

_____

_____

_____

What topics or types of information, if any, should never be discussed on social media?

_____

_____

_____

IF YOU CARE, SHARE!

Jews in All Hues is a grassroots organization dedicated to creating welcoming spaces for Jews of dual or multiple heritage. They use their Facebook page to share information about upcoming events and to get supporters' feedback on issues the organization is tackling, and also to raise awareness about the different faces of the Jewish community. For example, they often post about celebrities you may not have known are Jewish, personal reflections about integrating kimchi into their Passover Seder, or highlights of other organizations' efforts to support equality and inclusiveness in the Jewish community.

In addition to thinking about who will post and what topics are relevant, Jewish organizations may also want to address social media use on Shabbat and holidays. Check off the statement that best describes how your organization approaches social media engagement during those times.

←———————|—————————|—————————|—————————|—————————→

| We will actively post, comment, and respond. | We will only respond to comments, but not actively post. | We will only respond to timely issues or emergencies. | We will schedule content to be posted, but will not actively post. | We will not use social media in any way. |

How will you articulate your expectations of staff and/or volunteers who are using social media on behalf of your organization on Shabbat and holidays?

_____

_____

_____

_____

_____

_____

DARIM
ONLINE

Develop a Plan for Your Organization

Summarize your position on this topic (The language you use here can be the basis for your policy document).

_____

_____

_____

_____

_____

What other information do you need to gather?

_____

_____

_____

_____

_____

What other questions has this brought up that you need to address?

_____

_____

_____

_____

_____

DARIM
ONLINE

5. MONITORING POLICY

"Ben (the son of) Zoma said: Who is wise? He who learns from all people, as it is said: 'From all those who taught me I gained understanding' (Psalms 119:99)." Pirkei Avot 4:1.

Hopefully, people are talking about your organization, your community, and the issues you care about. Seeing and participating is a powerful way to engage your constituents, foster relationships, strengthen community, and build your brand. How much of the chatter you pay attention to happening in other people's online spaces and how closely your monitor your own online spaces is an important strategy decision.

Who Will Be Responsible?

Think about whose plate monitoring will fall on. Who will be responsible for monitoring external social media (other blogs, Facebook pages, Twitter accounts, etc.) and tracking mentions, questions and other relevant comments?

For your own channels, who's responsible for tracking and moderating comments, if not the person in charge of each?

When people write something to you or about you that deserves a response, what is a reasonable response time? What are your expectations of staff to monitor these channels in the evening and/or weekends or vacations? Should staff be instructed to respond or specifically not respond on Shabbat or holidays?

If others not primarily responsible for monitoring see something that should be paid attention to (positive or negative things...), whom should they inform?

THINKING ABOUT MONITORING

It can be difficult to weigh the amount of time you should spend monitoring. On one hand, if you aren't listening when someone is talking about you or your issues, you could miss an opportunity to make an important connection, provide support or defray a bad situation.

On the other hand, it can be time consuming to monitor everything, and every organization has a lot of priorities to juggle. The more effort you put in, the more results you'll turn up. You may need to question some assumptions of how you've structured job descriptions and time allocations. In some cases you may have one key person doing all the monitoring. In other cases you might delegate particular listening (these blogs, those keywords or issue areas) to various staff who work in those areas.

Think about where you will draw the line. What is important for you to know and what is overkill? How much effort you choose to invest should depend on the size of your organization (the bigger you are, the more likely it is that you'll be discussed), the volatility of your issue area, and the size of your online community (a bigger community is likely to necessitate more monitoring).

Think about your organizational values, as well. Are there values that would impact a decision on how responsive and engaged you need to be?

DARIM

What's Your Strategy?

Consider your own strategy, taking into account the factors in the Thinking About Monitoring box. Then check the box below that best describes how you would like monitoring to happen at your organization:

☐ We use listening to keep track of important mentions of our name, but it is not a priority for us.

☐ We listen in a few core ways to feel reasonably comfortable that we'll see it if we are mentioned. We understand that listening is important for us, but do not obsess over it.

☐ Listening is important to us for providing customer service and engagement of our key constituents.

☐ We listen actively to participate in our field, be in dialogue with our constituents, help make connections, and weave our network.

☐ We listen to everyone and everything that could possibly mention our organization in any way to can keep on top of all happenings in relation to our organization. Listening is how we know what to say.

"If someone tells you: 'I labored but didn't get results-' don't believe him. 'I did not labor, but got re-sults-' don't believe him. 'I labored and got results-' only then believe him." Talmud, Megillah 6b

It's important to recognize the tradeoff between time and results when it comes to measuring. In the chart below, mark the line where you would like to see your organization. Note that the hours you put in directly impact what you can get out of monitoring, so no cheating by deciding you're going to get all of the impact with none of the effort!

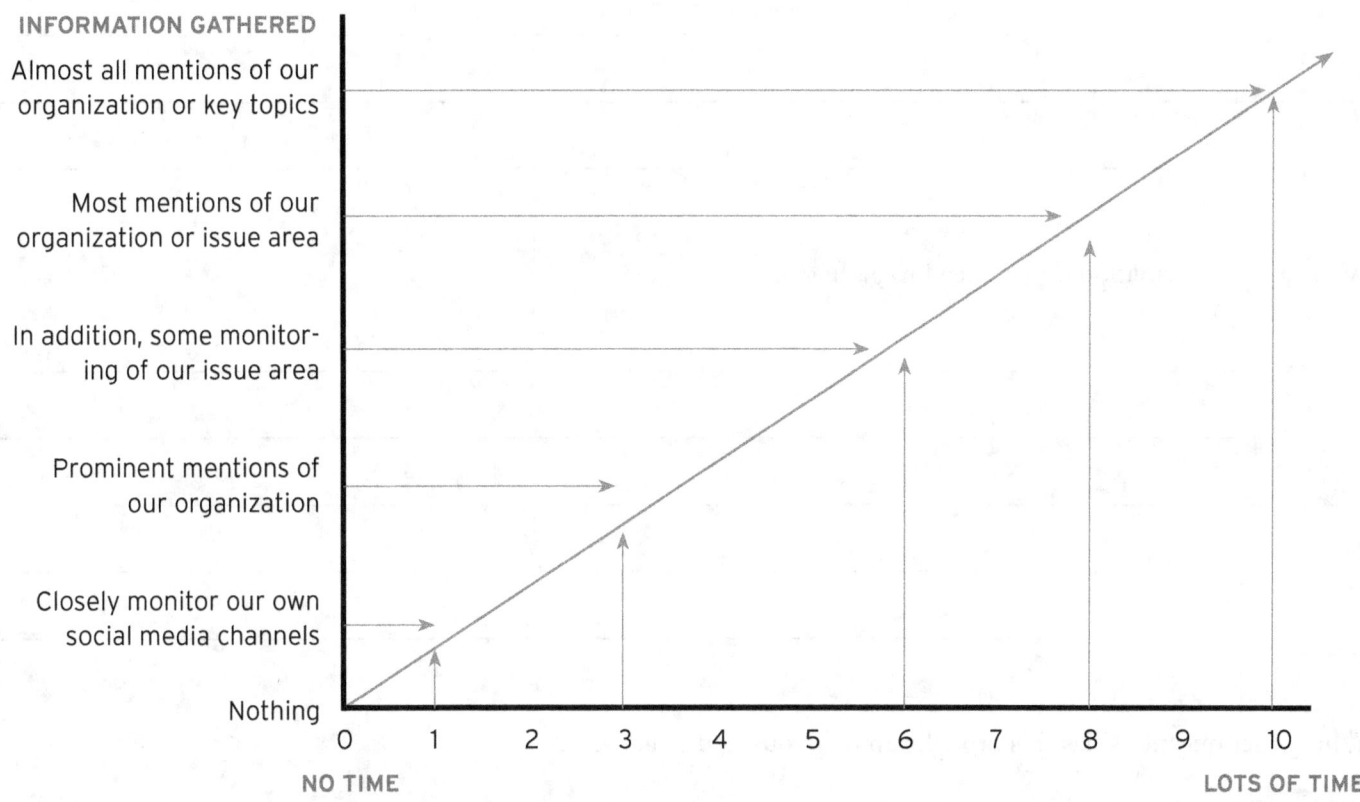

Write a statement describing what you plan to do in the world of monitoring—use the strategy language above, or craft your own.

_____

_____

_____

MONITORING YOUR FIELD, AS WELL AS YOUR ORGANIZATION

The Jewish Education Project, a large central agency, uses monitoring to keep track of important mentions of their organization and work. "We listen for the name of the organization, names of programs and events we offer, and mentions of staff and key leadership," says Associate Director of Marketing, Rebecca Saidlower. "Our department heads especially are considered thought leaders in their fields, and we want to keep up-to-date about any news regarding them and the work of their departments. We also encourage staff to keep track of those names, initiatives, and other key phrases that are important to their work." The organization also follows Twitter hashtags and blogs on Jewish education and innovation to keep abreast of important developments in that arena.

DARIM

Develop a Plan for Your Organization

Summarize your position on this topic (The language you use here can be the basis for your policy document).

_____

_____

_____

_____

_____

What other information do you need to gather?

_____

_____

_____

_____

What other questions has this brought up that you need to address?

_____

_____

_____

_____

6. RESPONDING TO NEGATIVE COMMENTS

"R. Yochanan said on the authority of R. Simeon b. Yochai: Verbal wrong is more heinous than monetary wrong. ... R. Samuel b. Nachmani said: For the latter restoration is possible, but not for the former." Talmud, Bava Metzia 58b.

When we jump into social media, we are acknowledging that we can never have perfect control over our message. Conversations are already happening about our work, as they always have–in the parking lot, at the grocery store, in people's living rooms, etc. Now social media makes some of those conversations visible, giving us the opportunity to participate in them and build relationships with the people who care most about our work.

Some people's first instinct is to delete anything negative. In some cases this may be appropriate, but keep in mind that public conversations can impact more than just the person who originally posted the comment. For the sake of education or building trust, it is worthwhile to consider how else you might handle the situation.

In addition to thinking about how you will respond on your own social media channels (e.g. your Facebook page), consider how you will respond to comments about your organization and its work or issue areas in social media spaces outside your "official" channels. Monitoring for these kinds of comments (see Worksheet #5) and responding to them thoughtfully can be a powerful mechanism for broadening your own awareness of your issue area, engaging in meaningful dialogue, educating people about your work, or setting the record straight.

Take time now to think through how you will respond (if at all) to even the most difficult comments in advance, and how you will advise your staff and volunteers, before these situations may arise.

SO SOMEONE SAYS SOMETHING BAD...
1. Could you turn a complaint into a conversation, an opportunity to learn or improve?
2. Does the post have misinformation about your work or issue area?
3. Will it damage your community?

DARIM

4. Does it include vulgarity, hate speech, or other purposefully inflammatory language? **IF YES** Consider whether you should respond carefully, not respond, remove it, or report it. You may want to also consider: Is the post from a person or group who has demonstrated this kind of behavior in the past? Who, if anyone, responds? What types of things do you say? Who needs to know about the post? For instance, if a comment has been deemed blatantly anti-Semitic, should it be reported?

5. Are they likely to keep posting objectionable things simply because you're responding? **IF YES** If none of the above were true, but they're likely to keep posting, it's almost certainly better not to respond.

EXAMPLE OF POSTING COMMUNITY GUIDELINES

National Jewish Health, a respiratory health hospital, maintains a presence in several social media spaces. On their website they've posted a set of commenting guidelines to set the standard for healthy engagement online. In the guidelines, National Jewish Health makes it clear what kinds of interactions are acceptable and which are off-limits and risk removal. "We also expect a basic level of civility; disagreements are fine, but mutual respect is a must, and profanity or abusive language are out-of-bounds." Their comments policy prohibits spam, commercial, and chain letter-style postings, warns users about copyright infringement, and alerts fans that positive comments may be used in future promotional materials for the organization. Publicly posting a set of community guidelines can help set the tone for your organization's online presence, and provide a useful safeguard should any issues arise.

http://www.nationaljewish.org/about/mediacenter/social-media/comment-policy/

A different national organization with a particularly controversial mission publicly posts what it expects of its community. They won't "discourage users from taking controversial positions or expressing vigorously what may be unpopular views," but they reserve the right to take action if posts are "reasonably construed as abusive, destructive, harmful, or threatening to the safety of others."

Develop a Plan for Your Organization

Summarize your position on this topic (The language you use here can be the basis for your policy document).

_____

_____

_____

_____

_____

What other information do you need to gather?

_____

_____

_____

_____

What other questions has this brought up that you need to address?

_____

_____

_____

_____

DARIM
ONLINE

7. RESPONDING TO POSITIVE AND NEUTRAL COMMENTS

"Much have I learned from my teachers, even more from my friends, most of all from my students."
Talmud, Taanit 7a.

So you're paying close attention to other people's posts on your own social media sites and listening to what other people are saying about you. If someone says something, when do you respond?

For each of the situations below, think how you'd want to respond. When would you simply ignore the post and not respond at all? When would you post a quick reply, and when would you write a more thoughtful response? Think about if and how your response might vary when someone posts in your spaces (e.g. a comment on your blog, or a post on your Facebook Page), versus when someone is talking about your work in other spaces (e.g. a post or comment on someone else's blog).

Reflect back on your initial values from Worksheet 1 and consider how they apply here. In some cases responding to positive and neutral comments may seem unnecessary or a burden on your time. However, if you're seeking to strengthen relationships, engage constituents more deeply, and build a sense of community, these are exactly the people for whom a response will have an important impact. Thus, being more proactive in your responding may in fact be a very efficient way to achieve these goals and embody your values.

ON YOUR OWN SOCIAL MEDIA CHANNELS:	Not reply at all	Post a quick stock reply	Write a thoughtful reply	Pull other people in for their insight or signoff	Other
If someone you don't know posts...					
A question for you					
A quick comment about your organization					
A thoughtful or detailed comment about your organization					

ON YOUR OWN SOCIAL MEDIA CHANNELS:	Not reply at all	Post a quick stock reply	Write a thoughtful reply	Pull other people in for their insight or signoff	Other
Other types of content:					
If a core supporter posts...					
A question for you					
A quick comment about your organization					
A thoughtful or detailed comment about your organization					
Other types of content:					
If _____ posts...(fill in other potential posters to consider)					
A question for you					
A quick comment about your organization					

DARIM
ONLINE

ON YOUR OWN SOCIAL MEDIA CHANNELS:	Not reply at all	Post a quick stock reply	Write a thoughtful reply	Pull other people in for their insight or signoff	Other
A thoughtful or detailed comment about your organization					
Other types of content:					

If _____ posts...(fill in other potential posters to consider)					
A question directed to you					
A quick comment about your organization					
A thoughtful or detailed comment about your organization					
Other types of content:					

DARIM
ONLINE

CREATING A POSITIVE SOCIAL MEDIA FORCE

For a large humanitarian organization, the goal of the social media policy was to create a positive force by guiding people and encouraging them in the right direction rather than providing a series of restrictions and limits. The senior communications director drafted it with that goal in mind.

"The guidelines are very much enabling," he said. "Those were the kinds of ideas we focused on. Because there are so many volunteers, social media should be a natural fit—it should be easy to empower them. I really wanted something which embraces that nature and steers the energy in the right direction. You can't guide what volunteers say, but you *can* ask them to think about what the organization would do, and make suggestions."

TEMPLE ISRAEL OF MEMPHIS

Temple Israel in Memphis, Tennessee uses their Facebook Page (https://www.facebook.com/TempleIsrael) to help make their large congregation feel more intimate. Temple Israel listens to their community on and off-line. So when the synagogue office heard that one Temple member had helped another older member change her flat tire, the staff shared the story through Facebook with a photo. Results: community members connected the names and faces with the story, the story contributed to building their culture of *mitzvot*, and it illustrated how the synagogue community lives both inside and outside of the building walls.

The warmth of the this community probably was apparent to Scott, a newcomer to Memphis, who posted on the Temple Israel Facebook page that he was new to the area and looking to meet some people. Iste Bardos, Communications Director, promptly replied, not only welcoming Scott to the area, but helping him achieve his goal by inviting him to a 20/30's event that week and connecting him with the young Assistant Rabbi.

"We use social media, especially Facebook and increasingly Twitter, to inform and engage in conversations. Reviewing the comments and posts every day is important for a number of reasons, but it can be boiled down to this: as with real-life conversations, there is a timely flow to online conversations. Quite simply, people appreciate prompt and honest responses. It shows you care, you're sincere, and they are important to you. That creates trust and an appreciation for one another," says Iste.

"Maya Angelou had it right when she said, 'I've learned that people will forget what you *said*, people will forget what you *did*, but people will never forget how you made them *feel*.' By responding to comments and online posts with swift sincerity, you are creating positive connections and feelings. And creating and maintaining positive and long-lasting relationships is what effective use of social media is about."

Develop a Plan for Your Organization

Summarize your position on this topic (The language you use here can be the basis for your policy document).

_____

_____

_____

_____

_____

What other information do you need to gather?

_____

_____

_____

_____

_____

What other questions has this brought up that you need to address?

_____

_____

_____

_____

_____

8. PRIVACY AND PERMISSIONS

"A base fellow gives away secrets, but a trustworthy soul keeps a confidence." Proverbs 11:13.

Social media venues are a great way to share information, but it's important to make sure that the information is yours to share. This is especially important for organizations that work in sensitive areas, such as schools or social service agencies, where legal boundaries or cultural expectations are particularly important.

Your organization likely already has a privacy policy. Now is the time to pull that out and determine how it can inform your decisions about your social media policy. You may want to reference your privacy policy and further take the opportunity to update your privacy policy to include use of personal information, photos and video in social media spaces.

While your organization may not have a culture of sharing photos, videos, names, or stories of people, you may want to consider how evolving that culture may benefit your mission and goals. Social media is, by definition, social. Determining how you can be as personal and social as possible, without compromising individuals' privacy, is an important exercise. If you are evolving an established practice, consider carefully how you may need to update waivers and educate your community about your new policies. (See information on waivers and permission forms below.)

WHEN CAN YOU POST:	Never	With Permission From Those Referenced	In private spaces (e.g. password protected blogs or closed Facebook groups)	Always–This is Not an Issue	Under These Circumstances
Photos or videos where individuals aren't identifiable?					
Photos or videos with clearly identifiable members, participants, volunteers, or other people you work with?					
Photos or videos with clearly identifiable staff, supporters, or other partners?					
Photos or videos with clearly identifiable members of your general community?					
Photos or videos with clearly identifiable children/minors?					
The full names of your staff, supporters, or other community members?					

DARIM
ONLINE

WHEN CAN YOU POST:	Never	With Permission From Those Referenced	In private spaces (e.g. password protected blogs or closed Facebook groups)	Always–This is Not an Issue	Under These Circumstances
Information, photos, or video about the services you've provided to specific constituents and/or community members.					
Someone's name associated with a photo or video (i.e. "tagging" them)?					
A location associated with a photo or video?					
Other					
Other					
Other					

For More on Privacy and Permissions

If you've selected the "With Permission From Those Referenced" category for any of your constituents, take a look at your organizational marketing waiver form for photos and videos if you have one—is social media included? If not, consider adding an additional clause. If you do not have a current marketing waiver form for photos and videos, refer to bit.ly/ypQ5IJ for help creating one.

If a third party posts something to one of your sites that seems to violate someone's privacy, you're not legally responsible for it (bit.ly/aUT4sQ). If you know that a post or photo might make someone uncomfortable, however, it's not a bad practice to take it down anyway.

The Children's Online Privacy Protection Act regulates the collection by entities under US jurisdiction of permission information from children under 13 years of age, and what responsibilities an operator has to protect children's privacy and safety online. It's worth familiarizing yourself with this law. Learn more about this Act on Wikipedia at http://bit.ly/childprivacyact.

KEEPING PRIVATE INFORMATION OFFLINE

For one human service organization, "privacy meant everything from getting permission to use photos and videos of clients to directing private conversations offline."

"For example, posts should be made regularly, but only by approved staff," the executive director said. "I never put up a post without running it by the management team—that's important, as it covers you and it covers the agency. Because our organization is a mental health organization that serves clients, we needed to make sure of the legal boundaries. Social media can blur those, and that's only appropriate to a point in certain communities. One example, clearly stated in the policy, is that staff should not engage in any kind of public discussion about private information online."

DARIM
ONLINE

Develop a Plan for Your Organization

Summarize your position on this topic (The language you use here can be the basis for your policy document).

_____

_____

_____

_____

_____

What other information do you need to gather?

_____

_____

_____

_____

_____

What other questions has this brought up that you need to address?

_____

_____

_____

_____

_____

DARIM
ONLINE

9. THINKING THROUGH COPYRIGHT AND ATTRIBUTION

"Anyone who says a statement in the name of the one who said it brings redemption to the world, as the verse says 'And Esther said to the King in the name of Mordechai' (Esther 2:22)." Pirkei Avot 6:6.

Nearly every *d'var Torah* ever given includes "as I learned from my teacher, _____." Jewish tradition reminds us to share wisdom learned from others and to credit our teachers and mentors. We encourage you to think about this as you determine how you will share and use content in your social media activities.

There are two sides to copyright and attribution issues. First, what are your policies for allowing other people to use your content? On the flip side, how will you use other people's content respectfully?

How Copyrighted is Your Content?

Are others allowed to use your content? Think through the considerations in the *How Do You Decide* box, and check the option below that applies to your organization:

Creative Commons (CC) is a non-profit organization devoted to expanding the range of creative works available for others to use and share legally. The organization has released several copyright licenses known as Creative Commons licenses, which allow creators to communicate which rights they reserve, and which rights they waive. The result is an agile (and free to use) copyright management system, which assists both creators and users of content. For more information, see the Creative Commons website at creativecommons.org to find the license version that matches your choices, and note it on your content.

If you've chosen a more open "Creative Commons" approach to your content, choose which of the following are important. Check all that apply:

☐ **Attribution:** If they repost, they should credit us for the content with a link back to our site.

☐ **Derivatives:** Anyone can modify our content as they like, and repost it, without needing permission.

☐ **Commercial Use:** Someone can use our content to sell something, without needing permission.

Check out the Creative Commons website at creativecommons.org to find the license version that matches your choices, and note it on your content.

HOW DO YOU DECIDE?

How copyrighted should your content be? Weigh the value of keeping full control over it—if others could do harm by using it, for instance—against the value of a more open sharing model.

A more open model lets your supporters promote your work on your behalf, which can have huge benefits. Unless you have a specific reason to reserve the rights to your content, it probably makes sense to allow others a little leeway to repost and distribute it.

Once you decide, put a note on each social media site as to what type of copyright or license you've decided on (the bottom of each page is typical). By default, if you don't label it, all your content is copyrighted—but it doesn't hurt to say so. If you'd like to use a more open license, make sure to let people know.

DARIM
ONLINE

How Are You Using Other People's Content?

You shouldn't assume that anything you can find online is fair game for you to use. If there's no indication of licensing on it, you have to assume that it's copyrighted—don't just pull it into your social media sites. It's always OK to link to something, but it's considered good courtesy to include an attribution to the original source.

How will you ensure that staff members aren't posting copyrighted information or photos, and are attributing photos and videos properly when required? Will you moderate? Spot check? Provide training?

_____

_____

_____

_____

When you post a link (for instance, on Twitter or Facebook), how will you indicate whose link it is? If you found the link through a third party, will you attribute them too? As an example, on Twitter you might say "Good @Idealware article: www.bit.ly/356677 (tip of the hat to @TechSoup)"

DARIM
ONLINE

Develop a Plan for Your Organization

Summarize your position on this topic (The language you use here can be the basis for your policy document).

_____

_____

_____

_____

_____

What other information do you need to gather?

_____

_____

_____

_____

_____

What other questions has this brought up that you need to address?

_____

_____

_____

_____

_____

DARIM
ONLINE

10. DRAWING THE LINE BETWEEN PERSONAL AND PROFESSIONAL

"Torah study is good with a worldly occupation, because the exertion put into both of them makes one forget sin." Pirkei Avot 2:2

"It has been taught: Rabbi Akiba said: Once I went in after Rabbi Joshua to a private place, and I learnt from him three things...Said Ben Azzai to him: Did you dare to take such liberties with your master? He replied: It was a matter of Torah, and I required to learn." -Berachot 62a

The line between personal and professional life has always been blurry for those working in the Jewish community; Jewish professionals are never really "off-duty." Social media further blends these already fuzzy distinctions. Though this is often a challenge, it is also an asset to Jewish organizations, as your employees may leverage their personal networks to amplify the organization's message. Many people today are much more comfortable blending their personal and professional lives in terms of content, platforms, and time. For example, one might post to friends on Facebook during the workday, and respond to professional tweets late
at night.

While there is often a concern that staff will spend too much time on social media for personal reasons (which is ultimately a management issue, not a social media issue), empowering your people to thoughtfully engage their personal networks on behalf of your cause is a powerful means of building relationships and amplifying your message.

There are several important pieces to consider in navigating this territory. For instance, will you ask staff to distinguish between their personal and professional presence online? And if so, how? Are there any key staff or leaders whose position is such that they need to take even further consideration of what they write personally (e.g. political advocacy on a rabbi's personal Twitter account that could jeopardize an employer's 501c3 status)? To what extent will you expect key staff to monitor professional social media channels outside of work hours? And will you set any boundaries about how much personal use can occur during the workday?

Ultimately, you may want to consider your organization's current culture and your vision for the future. How does the personal/professional blend (or divide) manifest itself now? How would you like to see this culture evolve? Your social media savvy staff and volunteers are key drivers to help you achieve this vision. Thus, engaging them in the articulation of how you want the culture to evolve will educate them, give them direction, and enable them to create the culture you seek. Intentionally developing a healthy balance between the personal and professional among your staff and volunteer teams will help them feel empowered and secure and help your organization expand its influence online.

Whatever your solution, it's important to lay out the ground rules ahead of time to ensure that all your staff—who may have very different ideas about what's appropriate - are clear about the expectations.

If you do advocacy work, keep in mind that there may be legal issues inherent in people advocating opinions on your behalf. Reference bit.ly/1dfHDv for more details.

Personal Overlapping Into the Professional

Where's the line between personal and professional in your organization? Think through the scenarios below.

WHAT?	Always OK	Never OK	OK in These Circumstances
Posting as the organization on the organization's page/account			
Posting personal things on the organization's site			
Announcing major life events of staff (such as birthdays, weddings, major awards, etc.)			
Personal opinion (unsigned)			
Personal opinion (signed)			
Posting as staff member on the organization's page/account			
Official organizational response			
Personal opinion			
Personal informational tidbits			
Posting as volunteer on the organization's page/account			
Official organizational response			
Personal opinion			
Personal informational tidbits			
Posting as individual on personal page/account			
Personal opinion about organization			

DARIM
ONLINE

WHAT?	Always OK	Never OK	OK in These Circumstances
Announcements about formal events or resources			
Comments about informal or internal happenings			
Connect with clients or other organizational constituents			

Professional Overlapping into the Personal

What can the organization request of staff in terms of their personal accounts? This is a difficult area. As an organization, do you actually have any right to define what certain staff should do with their personal accounts in their personal time? While you should never require someone to act a certain way or post certain things, it is important to identify some expectations and define boundaries for what you can request. Do any of the below apply?

☐ We might encourage staff to post organizational announcements on their personal account(s).

☐ We request that staff maintain a certain moral standard on their personal accounts.

☐ We'll monitor what staff say about the organization on personal accounts.

If you checked any of the boxes, describe your policy in more detail below. When does it apply?

PERSONAL AND PROFESSIONAL BOUNDARIES

One of the thorniest areas of policy faced by the family service agency was that of personal and professional boundaries. Even if staff don't self-identify on their individual Twitter feeds or Facebook profiles as employees, in most cases, a good number of people still know where they work—it's difficult to keep those worlds completely separate.

"Personal online posts should be consistent with [the organization's] mission," the program director said. "There has to be a decision, whether you agree with that solution or not, about whether you feel it's necessary to dictate how personal pages reflect the organization. It needs to be clear to employees what that separation is. You can't discuss all the specific situations, but you need to consider broader statements that will cover them."

Develop a Plan for Your Organization

Summarize your position on this topic (The language you use here can be the basis for your policy document).

_____

_____

_____

_____

_____

What other information do you need to gather?

_____

_____

_____

_____

_____

What other questions has this brought up that you need to address?

_____

_____

_____

_____

_____

DARIM
ONLINE

SAMPLE POLICY LANGUAGE

Introduction

As you develop your own social media policy or guideline, it is often helpful to see how other organizations have addressed the same challenges and opportunities. That's not to say that you should simply copy and paste your way to a policy. Involving your colleagues in conversations and discussions about wording will help you evolve your culture and understand the implications of your decisions and actions. But drawing inspiration from examples of other organizations language can be very helpful. In some cases, similar wording could even be just the right thing for your organization.

The following sections correspond to the sections of the Social Media Policy Workbook for Jewish Organizations. Notice we have included multiple examples in each section to help you see the range of ways to approach each aspect of your policy. Also notice how in some places you see "don't" language (top down feel), and in others you see "let's do…" (encouraging and inclusive feel). This varies by the area of the policy, the culture of the organization, and the actions they are seeking to influence. You may find it useful to pursue the links to the full policy to see the context of the quoted language shown here, or to view other aspects of their social media policy.

1. What Does A Social Media Policy Mean To You?

Different organizations can have very different policies. In practice, "social media policy" could refer to a detailed set of procedures for using social media, a legal document written by lawyers, a high-level vision document, or pretty much anything inbetween. What kind of social media policy do you want to create?

YMCA of METROPOLITAN DALLAS Social Networking Policy
http://www.campgradyspruce.org/images/upload/Social%20Media%20Policy.pdf

> *The YMCA recognizes the importance of the Internet in shaping public thinking about our organization and our current and potential services. We also recognize the importance of our employees joining in and helping shape industry conversation and direction through interaction in social media. The YMCA is committed to supporting honest, transparent, and knowledgeable dialogue on the Internet through social media.*

FRATERNAL ORDER OF EAGLES Social Media Guidelines
http://www.foe.com/pdf/eagle-space/social-media-guidelines.pdf

> *The Grand Aerie encourages local, regional, district, state aeries and auxiliaries, and clubs-within-a-club to use any tool available to increase membership, communicate with members and potential members, fundraise, and increase positive exposure. To that end, social media sites such as You Tube, MySpace, Twitter, and Facebook and others should be embraced and used with the guidelines set by the Grand Aerie. Social media sites allow you to connect to members and potential members in a very interactive way. The sites allow you to share video, post information, show pictures, promote your Aerie and F.O.E. charities, receive feedback, and best of all, network.*
>
> *As with anything, we need to take some precautions when using social media tools connected with our organization. The same resources that make social media attractive are also the same elements that can injure the perception of the Fraternal Order of Eagles.*
>
> *The following social media guidelines are for any internet based, unofficial Fraternal Order of Eagles site or otherwise related online unofficial internet based element to The Fraternal Order of Eagles. If you build a website not using the CMS tools, create a Facebook, My Space or other site/page and use any Fraternal Order of Eagles logo or related image or name your page/site as the resource of information for your aerie/auxiliary or other entity of the Fraternal Order of Eagles, you have created an unofficial internet based element and must comply with the following guidelines.*

2. Your Organization's Social Media Values

Your social media policy should not live in a vacuum, but should be guided by the values and mission of your organization. Here's how a few articulate their values via their policies.

THE BOY SCOUTS OF AMERICA Social Media Guidelines
http://www.scouting.org/scoutsource/Marketing/Resources/SocialMedia.aspx

> *Be Scout-like. When disagreeing with others' opinions, remain appropriate and polite. If you find yourself in a situation online that looks as if it's becoming antagonistic, do not get overly defensive and do not disengage from the conversation abruptly. Ask your Scout executive or the designee for advice on how to disengage from the dialogue in a polite manner that reflects well on the BSA.*

> *Build trust by being open and transparent. Share information and what the challenges and opportunities are for Scouting in your community.*

THE COCA-COLA COMPANY Online Social Media Principles
http://www.viralblog.com/wp-content/uploads/2010/01/TCCC-Online-Social-Media-Principles-12-2009.pdf

> *The vision of the Company to achieve sustainable growth online and offline is guided by certain shared values that we live by as an organization and as individuals:*

> - *LEADERSHIP: The courage to shape a better future;*
>
> - *COLLABORATION: Leveraging our collective genius;*
>
> - *INTEGRITY: Being real;*
>
> - *ACCOUNTABILITY: Recognizing that if it is to be, it's up to me;*
>
> - *PASSION: Showing commitment in heart and mind;*
>
> - *DIVERSITY: Being as inclusive as our brands; and*
>
> - *QUALITY: Ensuring what we do, we do well.*

> *These Online Social Media Principles are intended to outline how these values should be demonstrated in the online social media space and to guide your participation in this area, both when you are participating personally, as well as when you are acting on behalf of the Company.*

THE AMERICAN INSTITUTE OF ARCHITECTS Policy on Staff Use of Social Media

http://www.aia.org/about/AIAB083034

Matter of Trust

Being able to share your and the AIA's activities without prior management approval means the Institute trusts you to understand that by doing so you are accepting a higher level of risk for greater rewards ... Trust is an essential ingredient in the constructive culture we are striving to achieve at the AIA. We can't be there to guide every interaction, so we expect you to follow these guidelines and advice to help you better balance the risk vs. reward ratio.

NORDSTROM Social Networking Guidelines

http://shop.nordstrom.com/c/social-networking-guidelines

Be Humble

Our number-one goal is to offer each customer great service, but we're certainly not perfect and we do make mistakes. Let's stay focused on working to deliver great service instead of bragging about it.

3. Social Media Roles: Who Does What?

Determining who's in charge of each of your social media activities is essential to assigning responsibility and accountability throughout your organization. When clear roles are defined, your organization can more easily execute strategy and understand who can—and who cannot—do what.

POWERHOUSE MUSEUM Internet/Intranet Usage Policy
http://www.powerhousemuseum.com/pdf/about/policies/Internet_Intranet_policy.pdf

The Official Museum Presence on Social Media

The Museum maintains several Facebook pages and groups, Twitter accounts, Flickr accounts and groups, as well as accounts on YouTube, Vimeo, BlipTV, Slideshare and other sites.

All official social media accounts are managed by the Web and Social Technologies team in the Digital, Social and Emerging Technologies Department. The Manager, Web and Social Technologies, is responsible for the security of passwords and upkeep of these accounts. The Manager, Web and Social Technologies, grants access to other members of staff to administer groups on the platforms and to post content.

Access is granted on a project-by-project basis and in discussion with Head, Digital, Social and Emerging Technologies and only following project approval by the Museum Executive. Access to the Museum's Flickr accounts also requires approval by Manager, Visual and Digitization Services. Staff who are granted access to post or create content in an official capacity must have undergone supervision and, where required, training in appropriate conduct specific to each platform. This access can be revoked by Manager, Web and Social Technologies at any time.

BREAD FOR THE WORLD Social Media Policy
http://www.socialmedia.biz/social-media-policies/bread-for-the-worlds-social-media-policy/

...and whenever possible, we will be supportive of social media sites initiated by Bread's grassroots. If needed, we shall provide them with the help to bring their sites up to Bread's standards. These sites, however, shall carry a disclaimer that they were set up by Bread members and activists and are not official Bread sites. As the liaison to Bread's grassroots, the Organizing Department will provide support for these sites, including notification of changes in messaging.

JEWISH FAMILY SERVICE OF BERGEN AND NORTH HUDSON Social Media Policy

Establishing a JSF presence on a public social network (Twitter, Facebook, YouTune, LinkedIn, etc.) must be authorized beforehand by the Executive Director.

4. What Should You Say Online?

What should your staff be posting and sharing online? What topics should they never post about?

INTERNATIONAL FEDERATION OF RED CROSS AND RED CRESCENT SOCIETIES Social Media
Guidelines for IFRC Staff
http://sm4good.com/wp-content/uploads/2009/11/Red-Cross-Red-Crescent-SocialMedia-Guidelines.pdf

Think of CNN, your mother and your boss

Don't say anything online that you wouldn't be comfortable seeing quoted on CNN, being asked about by your mother or having to justify to your boss.

Add value

The IFRC believes that sharing of information and experiences benefits the whole humanitarian community and ultimately the beneficiaries we serve. Feel free to share and discuss your experiences in campaigns, field communication, building of transitional shelters etc. If IFRC staff is perceived to be knowledgeable and helpful this will reflect positively on you and on the organization. Obviously, use common sense where information is concerned that is internal and/or confidential. If in doubt - ask the owner of the information you want to share. Refrain from commenting on the work of colleagues in this or other organizations that are outside your field of expertise.

Spread the word and connect with your colleagues

Don't only talk about yourself but also about the successes of your colleagues. Connect with them through social networks and spread their success stories.

WALKER ART CENTER Blog Guidelines
http://newmedia.walkerart.org/nmiwiki/pmwiki.php/Main/WalkerBlogGuidelines

- *Use blogs to post material related to your department. Use Off Center to post about the art world in general.*

- *Use Walker blogs to track areas of research interest, web sites about a particular topic, or happenings in a particular field. Use the blogs as a tool to point to related material on the Walker's website as well as external sites.*

- *Use the blogs to engage audiences in a different way by providing a behind the scenes view of what makes our programming possible.*

- *Use Walker blogs to discuss Walker programming, post reviews, promote upcoming events, and receive comments.*

DARIM
ONLINE

THE AVI CHAI FOUNDATION Social Media Policy
http://jewpoint0.org/2011/04/avi-chai-foundation-gets-social/

Write What You Know. You have a unique perspective on our organization based on your talents, skills and current responsibilities. Share your knowledge, your passions and your personality in your posts by writing about what you know. If you're interesting and authentic, you'll attract readers who understand your specialty and interests. Don't spread gossip, hearsay or assumptions.

JUNIOR URBAN ADVENTURE Technology Guidelines
http://juniorurbanadventure.blogspot.com/2006/10/jua-technology-guidelines.html

Have something to say.
Having ideas and wondering things is perhaps the most powerful thing you can learn to do. Talking about your ideas in a public forum forces your ideas to grow, evolve and get better. Your ideas matter.

Stand on the shoulders of giants.
You have access to literally millions of other ideas. Read them, use them, be informed by them. Most critically - give people credit when you are influenced by them! Not only is stealing other people's ideas, words and images a form of academic dishonesty it's also simply wrong. Provide a link to the original content and use the author's name whenever possible.

Share your opinion.
Remember, what you have to say matters. Read the work of others and let them know what you think! When sharing your ideas, commenting on others and posting content, keep it clean. Use normal language that you would be fine in a public forum like school meeting. The same thing goes for images, audio and images. Disagreements are central to growing your ideas, but don't attack anyone personally.

Be safe.
There are creeps online just like in the real world. Don't publicly post anything you wouldn't tell a stranger on the street. Opinions and ideas belong in a public forum, your last name, passwords or phone number do not! In particular do not post the location of our lodging while we are in Boston. Use only your first name and last initial while blogging.

DARIM
ONLINE

5. Monitoring Policy

Hopefully, people are talking about your organization and the issues you care about. How much of the chatter you pay attention to is an important strategy decision.

COUNTY OF ORANGE County Social Media Use Policy and Procedure
http://cams.ocgov.com/Web_Publisher/Agenda05_18_2010_files/images/000610-000108A.PDF

> *Agency/Department social media sites shall be monitored regularly and prompt corrective action shall be taken when an issue arises that places, or has potential to place, the County at risk... Agency/Department social media site administrators shall review site activity and content daily for exploitation or misuse.*

THE BOY SCOUTS OF AMERICA Social Media Guidelines
http://www.scouting.org/scoutsource/Marketing/Resources/SocialMedia.aspx

> *Social media must be monitored. A qualified staff member or volunteer should have the responsibility of monitoring social media channels daily, and backup administrators/monitors should be designated so there is no gap in the monitoring.*

THE COCA-COLA COMPANY Online Social Media Principles
http://www.viralblog.com/wp-content/uploads/2010/01/TCCC-Online-Social-Media-Principles-12-2009.pdf

> *Be a "scout" for compliments and criticism. Even if you are not an official online spokesperson for the Company, you are one of our most vital assets for monitoring the social media landscape. If you come across positive or negative remarks about the Company or its brands online that you believe are important, consider sharing them by forwarding them to online.relations@ na.ko.com*

LAKE FOREST UNIVERSITY Social Media Guidelines
http://www.lakeforest.edu/offices/communications/socialmedia/students.php

> ### Consistently monitor your sites.
> *The key to social media success is to stay on top of your sites. Any social media site will require daily monitoring. Encourage discussion by posting quality content and questions. Quickly address any inappropriate messages or misuse. Such inappropriate content includes spam, advertising, offensive statements, inaccurate information, foul language, or unconstructive criticism of the College or anyone in the College community. An example of unconstructive criticism might be: "The food at the Caf stinks." A constructive criticism, on the other hand, might look like this: "The bagels in the caf are rock hard and need to be replaced."*
>
> *Social media can be used in as many productive ways as it can be misused. As a general guideline, if you have any question as to whether something should be removed, please contact the Communications Office. Please notify the Communications and Marketing Office when you do remove seriously inappropriate content.*

DARIM
ONLINE

Presence and Maintenance

Be present and responsive, and you will gain credibility and value. If you have a social media outpost and someone finds you, they may engage with you and expect a response. It could be a prospective student asking about an application deadline or a parent asking for the schedule of an event. Establishing and then deserting a social media outpost could reflect poorly on the university.

Tip: Software applications such as Tweetdeck and Seesmic can help you organize your use and monitoring of Twitter. You can set up Google Blog Alerts by keyword. Also, services like Social Mention allow you to monitor multiple social media services at once.

Be sure to monitor replies and comments. Check at least once a day and respond promptly.

DARIM
ONLINE

6. Responding to Negative Comments

It's hard to figure out when and how you should respond to a post about you, or on your own social media sites. Always? Never? What should you say?

THE BOY SCOUTS OF AMERICA Social Media Guidelines
http://www.scouting.org/scoutsource/Marketing/Resources/SocialMedia.aspx

- *Social media takes a thick skin. Negative conversations are happening already, but now you have a voice in the conversation. Don't delete negative comments unless they violate the terms laid out in the BSA Social Media Digital Contract.*

- *Be prepared to respond to negative or inaccurate posts if response is warranted. Some negative comments do not require a response, while others should be taken seriously and addressed. Factors such as the number of followers and the severity of the conversations should temper if and how you respond.*

- *Direct media inquiries to the appropriate person. Media inquiries coming through social media should be referred to the Scout executive or a designee for an official response.*

- *Be Scout-like. When disagreeing with others' opinions, remain appropriate and polite. If you find yourself in a situation online that looks as if it's becoming antagonistic, do not get overly defensive and do not disengage from the conversation abruptly. Ask your Scout executive or the designee for advice on how to disengage from the dialogue in a polite manner that reflects well on the BSA.*

- *Build trust by being open and transparent. Share information and what the challenges and opportunities are for Scouting in your community.*

SEATTLE UNIVERSITY Social Media Policy
http://www.seattleu.edu/marcom/Inner.aspx?id=53083

A healthy dialog with constructive criticism can be useful but refrain from engaging in dialogue that could disparage colleagues, competitors, or critics.

CISCO Social Media Guidelines
http://www.slideshare.net/CiscoSystems/cisco-social-media-guidelines-june-2010

If a reader leaves a negative comment, it is recommend that you do not delete the comment for transparency reasons. If the comment contains disrespectful or derogatory language you may consider NOT posting it. We do encourage that you publish most comments because it encourages people with different viewpoints and opinions to join the conversation, to debtate, and to discuss their side of a specific argument.

Receiving a negative comment about a Cisco product or service ultimately provides an oppor-
tunity to respond to the negative comment and reframe it in a positive light. Remember: more
often than not, the negative commenters are trying to provoke a response. Check with your
manager or a PR representative if you are unsure how to respond.

TUFTS UNIVERSITY Social Media Best Practices and Guidelines
http://webcomm.tufts.edu/?pid=25

If users post criticisms of your interest or organization, do not outright delete or suppress such
postings if they are valid points to consider. Let the comments stand. Correct misinformation,
but don't engage in heated arguments. Often, the community will correct itself and step in to
correct inaccuracies or defend the institution. If this happens and is sufficient to resolve the
issue, there may be no need for an additional official response.

Feel free to delete irrelevant or vulgar posts.

If you feel a post is threatening in nature or otherwise meriting greater concern, contact Web
Communications for advice.

DARIM

7. Responding to Positive and Neutral Comments

So you're paying close attention to other people's posts on your own social media sites and listening to what other people are saying about you. If someone says something, when do you respond?

THE BOY SCOUTS OF AMERICA Social Media Guidelines
http://www.scouting.org/scoutsource/Marketing/Resources/SocialMedia.aspx

- *Direct media inquiries to the appropriate person. Media inquiries coming through social media should be referred to the Scout executive or a designee for an official response.*

- *Build trust by being open and transparent. Share information and what the challenges and opportunities are for Scouting in your community.*

SOCIAL CAPITAL MANAGEMENT: Social Media Guidelines for Your Business and Nonprofit
http://socialcapitalmanagement.org/social-media-guidelines-for-your-business-and-non-profit-organization/

Keep a friendly and professional tone when posting updates and having conversations with supporters or customers. Avoid communicating in "corporate" tone.

When posting or replying to a message, take the time to review the content to ensure it cannot be interpreted in any negative light. And you should reply to comments in a timely manner if a response is needed.

TUFTS UNIVERSITY Social Media Best Practices and Guidelines
http://webcomm.tufts.edu/?pid=25

Presence and Maintenance
- *Be present and responsive, and you will gain credibility and value. If you have a social media outpost and someone finds you, they may engage with you and expect a response. It could be a prospective student asking about an application deadline or a parent asking for the schedule of an event. Establishing and then deserting a social media outpost could reflect poorly on the university.*

  - *Tip: Software applications such as Tweetdeck and Seesmic can help you organize your use and monitoring of Twitter. You can set up Google Blog Alerts by keyword. Also, services like Social Mention allow you to monitor multiple social media services at once.*

- *Be sure to monitor replies and comments. Check at least once a day and respond promptly.*

JUNIOR URBAN ADVENTURE Technology Guidelines
http://juniorurbanadventure.blogspot.com/2006/10/jua-technology-guidelines.html

Share your opinion.
Remember, what you have to say matters. Read the work of others and let them know what you think! When sharing your ideas, commenting on others and posting content, keep it clean. Use normal language that you would be fine in a public forum like school meeting. The same thing goes for images, audio and images. Disagreements are central to growing your ideas, but don't attack anyone personally.

8. Privacy and Permissions

Social media venues are a great way to share information, but it's important to make sure that the information is yours to share. This is especially important for organizations that work in sensitive areas, such as medical or healthcare environments, in which something as simple as a person's name or photo might carry an implication or association with your organization. What should your policies be in this area?

YMCA of METROPOLITAN DALLAS Social Networking Policy
http://www.campgradyspruce.org/images/upload/Social%20Media%20Policy.pdf

> *Employees should respect the privacy rights of their co-workers and must not disclose information about work-related events involving other employees of the YMCA, its clients, vendors and business partners without obtaining their permission. Employees must not post photographs or images of any co-workers, YMCA clients, vendors, or business partners on any social media site without having their express permission to do so.*

MAYO CLINIC Participation Guidelines For Mayo Clinic Employees
http://sharing.mayoclinic.org/guidelines/for-mayo-clinic-employees/

> *Mayo Clinic strongly discourages "friending" of patients on social media websites. Staff in patient care roles generally should not initiate or accept friend requests except in unusual circumstances such as the situation where an in-person friendship pre-dates the treatment relationship.*

> *Mayo Clinic discourages staff in management/supervisory roles from initiating "friend" requests with employees they manage. Managers/supervisors may accept friend requests if initiated by the employee, and if the manager/supervisor does not believe it will negatively impact the work relationship.*

INTERNATIONAL FEDERATION OF RED CROSS AND RED CRESCENT SOCIETIES Social Media Guidelines for IFRC Staff
http://sm4good.com/wp-content/uploads/2009/11/Red-Cross-Red-Crescent-SocialMedia-Guidelines.pdf

> ### Protect your own privacy
> *A lot of web sites allow you some form of control over who can see your material. Use these features. Example: On Facebook you can control your privacy settings under "Settings -> Privacy Settings -> Profile". We recommend that you set all of these settings except for "Profile" and "Basic info" to "Only friends."*

DEPAUL UNIVERSITY Social Media Guidelines
http://brandresources.depaul.edu/vendor_guidelines/g_post.aspx

Be thoughtful.

If you have any questions about whether it is appropriate to write about certain kinds of material in your role as a DePaul employee, ask your supervisor before you post. Remember that policies such as FERPA apply to social media.

TUFTS UNIVERSITY Social Media Best Practices and Guidelines
http://webcomm.tufts.edu/?pid=25

Confidentiality and Security

- *Do not post confidential or proprietary information about Tufts, its students, its alumni or your fellow employees. Use ethical judgment and follow university policies and federal requirements, such as FERPA.*

- *Do not collect sensitive information—such as phone numbers, student ID numbers, Social Security numbers, payment information, etc.—via social media, as those are not secure channels.*

- *If you discuss a situation involving individuals on a social media site, be sure that they cannot be identified.*

- *As a guideline, don't post anything that you would not present at a conference.*

CHILDREN'S HOSPITAL OF LOS ANGELES Share Your Story Use and Access
http://www.chla.org/site/?c=ipINKTOAJsG&b=5245675

What We May Do With the Information You Share With Us: By providing your story to us on this site, you authorize us to use your story in both online and offline formats, including but not limited to:

- *Any websites owned or managed by our hospital*

- *Social networking or social media platforms*

- *Presentations to supporters*

- *Brochures, direct mail, publications, etc.*

- *Video footage featuring our care for children*

DARIM
ONLINE

9. Thinking through Copyright and Attribution

There are two sides to copyright and attribution issues. First, what are your policies for allowing other people to use your content? On the flip side, how will you use other people's content respectfully?

JUNIOR URBAN ADVENTURE Technology Guidelines

http://juniorurbanadventure.blogspot.com/2006/10/jua-technology-guidelines.html

> ***Stand on the shoulders of giants.***
> *You have access to literally millions of other ideas. Read them, use them, be informed by them. Most critically - give people credit when you are influenced by them! Not only is stealing other people's ideas, words and images a form of academic dishonesty it's also simply wrong. Provide a link to the original content and use the author's name whenever possible.*

BREAD FOR THE WORLD Social Media Policy

http://www.socialmedia.biz/social-media-policies/bread-for-the-worlds-social-media-policy/

> ***...we will respect copyright rules.*** *We will properly cite our sources, and post only items that are covered by fair use or published under Creative Commons. Otherwise, we will seek permission first.*

BALL STATE UNIVERISTY Social Media Policy

http://cms.bsu.edu/About/AdministrativeOffices/UMC/WhatWeDo/Web/~/media/
DepartmentalContent/UMC/pdfs/BallState_SocialMediaPolicy.ashx

> ***Photography:***
> *Photographs posted on social media sites easily can be appropriated by visitors. Consider adding a watermark and/or posting images at 72 dpi and approximately 800x600 resolution to protect your intellectual property. Images at that size are sufficient for viewing on the Web, but not suitable for printing. Remember that the policies of Ball State University Photographic Services related to purchasing and using their images apply online as well as in print. Contact Photographic Services at 765-285-1571 with questions.*

NATIONAL PUBLIC RADIO Ethics Handbook

http://ethics.npr.org/?s=social+media

> *When posting or gathering material online, consider terms of service. It's important to keep in mind that the terms of service of a social media site apply to what we post there and to the information we gather from it. Also: The terms might allow for our material to be used in a*

different way than intended. Additionally, law enforcement officials may be able to obtain our reporting on these sites by subpoena without our consent — or perhaps even our knowledge. Social media is a vital reporting resource for us, but we must be vigilant about keeping work that may be sensitive in our own hands.

DEPAUL UNIVERSITY Social Media Guidelines
http://brandresources.depaul.edu/vendor_guidelines/g_post.aspx

> ***Respect trademarks and copyright.*** *This is usually part of the terms of service for the social media site you are using as well as part of DePaul's Acceptable Use Policy. You can use the university's logo on an official university social media site; contact University Marketing Communications to get a logo optimized for the site you are using. Photographs also are copyrighted, including those commissioned by the university (see the policy on Use of EM&M Marketing Photographs). You should only post photos you have taken yourself or have permission from the photographer to use.*

DARIM
ONLINE

10. Personal vs. Professional

Social media forces us to address difficult questions about the different ways our personal lives and professional work can intersect. Navigating between them can be difficult, especially on tools like Facebook that require the user to have a personal account to use an organization's page. It's important to lay out the ground rules ahead of time to ensure that all your staff—who may have very different idea about what's appropriate—are clear about the expectations.

INTERNATIONAL FEDERATION OF RED CROSS AND RED CRESCENT SOCIETIES Social media guidelines for IFRC staff
http://sm4good.com/wp-content/uploads/2009/11/Red-Cross-Red-Crescent-SocialMedia-Guidelines.pdf

While communication through social media networks is primarily a personal matter, this is not the same as it being private. In a lot of cases, written conversations inside these networks can be found through search engines such as Google. Even in cases where only your contacts can see what you write, there is a possibility that one of them will forward what you say and make it visible to a wider audience. As a result, personal conversation within social media networks should be considered public rather than private.

*... **Use a disclaimer***

If you have a blog and talk about work-related issues, add a disclaimer to each page making clear that the views you express are yours alone. Be aware that this disclaimer doesn't free you from the obligations you have under the Codes of Conduct or the Fundamental principles.

Example: "The postings on this site are my own and don't necessarily represent positions, strategies or opinions of my employer." If you have an "about me" page, we advise against using photos where you stand in front of one of the emblems since this might give the web site or blog an official appearance.

NATIONAL PUBLIC RADIO Ethics Handbook: Social Media
http://ethics.npr.org/tag/social-media/

Our standards of impartiality also apply to social media.

Refrain from advocating for political or other polarizing issues online. This extends to joining online groups or using social media in any form (including your Facebook page or a personal blog). Don't express personal views on a political or other controversial issue that you could not write for the air or post on NPR.org. These guidelines apply whether you are posting under your own name or — if the online site allows pseudonyms — your identity would not be readily apparent. In reality, anything you post online reflects both on you and on NPR.

Your simple participation in some online groups could be seen to indicate that you endorse

their views. Consider whether you can accomplish your purposes by just observing a group's activity, rather than becoming a member. If you do join, be clear that you've done so to seek information or story ideas. And if you "friend" or join a group representing one side of an issue, do so for groups representing other viewpoints.

AMERICAN SPEECH LANGUAGE HEARING ASSOCIATION Social Media Guidelines
http://beth.typepad.com/files/asha-social-media-guidelines.pdf

When staff communicates through social media, unless authorized to speak on behalf of ASHA, they are representing themselves … Use a disclaimer. If you write anything related to your work at ASHA on a blog or some other online space, make it clear that what you say there is representative of your views and opinions and you are not presenting yourself as a spokesperson for ASHA. Use a disclaimer such as: " "I am an employee at the American Speech-Language-Hearing Association; however this is my personal opinion." or something to that effect. Of course, this would only apply to writings that mention ASHA business-related topics.

FELLOWSHIP CHURCH Blogging Policy
http://www.leaveitbehind.com/home/2005/04/fellowship_chur.html

Respect Our Beliefs. *When working for a church, it is important to remember that employment decisions will be made based upon our Christian beliefs. If your personal website displays inappropriate images or reflects personal opinions or life-style choices that are contrary to Fellowship Church's religious beliefs, you may be subject to discipline, up to and including immediate termination of employment. For this reason, we encourage you to first seek guidance from your supervisor or Human Resources if you have any questions.*

Notify Your Supervisor. *If you currently have a personal website or weblog, or are considering starting one, be sure to discuss this with your supervisor. Also, if you have any questions, feel free to share them with HR or the Web Department.*

Include a Disclaimer. *On your site, please make it clear to your readers that the views you express are yours alone and that they do not necessarily reflect the views of Fellowship Church. To help reduce the potential for confusion, we recommend you prominently display the following notice, or something similar, on the homepage of your site:*

> *I work at Fellowship Church. Everything here, however, is my personal opinion and is not read or approved before it is posted. Opinions, conclusions and other information expressed here do not necessarily reflect the views of Fellowship Church.*

YMCA of METROPOLITAN DALLAS Social Networking Policy
http://www.campgradyspruce.org/images/upload/Social%20Media%20Policy.pdf

Employees should not use social media sites to monitor existing employees or screen or evaluate potential candidates for employment. Social media sites may reveal protected characteristics regarding potential candidates that may not be used in making employment decisions. Employees should not engage in any deceptive practices to obtain private information or use any obtained information in a discriminating manner.

Employees should not engage in any online conduct which: creates a conflict of interest between them and the YMCA, creates a conflict with one of the YMCA's program participants, or otherwise harms the business interests of the YMCA.

Employees may not give out their personal email addresses or links to their personal social networking profiles, blogs or websites to program participants. Employees may not initiate contact with program participants through any means of Internet communications outside of official, sanctioned YMCA communications.

If an adult program participant finds a staff member's personal social networking profile and requests to be linked as a friend, the employee may accept or deny the request at the employee's discretion.

If a minor program participant (any program participant under the age of 18) finds a staff member's personal social networking profile and requests to be linked as a friend, the employee must respectfully deny the request and block them from further contact. Employees must contact their supervisor if a minor program participant attempts to contact them through the Internet.

WEST SUBURBAN YMCA Social Networking Policy
http://www.westsuburbanymca.org/uploads/uploads/Files/Social%20Networking%20Policy.pdf

The YMCA does not intend to interfere with any employee's private life, but publicly observable communications, actions or words are not private. All YMCA staff must use good judgment and discretion. If you want your use of technology to be private, do not allow it to be seen in the electronic public forum. If you or your words are public, make sure they are not contradicting with your role at the YMCA and they are reflective of the mission and values of our association.

CONCLUSION

Pat yourself on the back. You've made it to the end of the Workbook! We hope these worksheets have helped you to refine your organization's thoughts about how you're using social media, and to define what is and isn't appropriate. Now that you've done the thinking, take the time to write up your policy or guideline, pass it through the appropriate approval processes and call it official.

The real work, however, comes in bringing this policy to life. Implementing the values, evolving the culture, empowering your staff and community to use these tools responsibly, and keeping your policy up to date over time as the tools, uses and your culture evolve. This should be a living document, so make sure to continue to keep it alive in conversation and used throughout your work.

We know this isn't a simple process, and that it's useful to hear what others are doing, and how it's going. If you're interested in learning from others who are working on their social media policy, we invite you to join the discussion in the Social Media Policy Facebook group at https://www.facebook.com/groups/socialmediapolicy/. You're welcome to post questions and respond to others. We are also eager to see what you've put together. Please share snippets of your policy, or post the whole thing online and share a link in the group so we can all learn from your work.

Thanks again to our authors, sponsors, reviewers, contributors, and to the entire Darim and Idealware communities for sharing your stories, work, questions and energy to make this Workbook a reality.

Lisa Colton, President, Darim Online

Miriam Brosseau, Special Projects Coordinator, Darim Online

Join us at http://www.facebook.com/darimonline

Follow us at http://www.twitter.com/darimonline

DARIM
ONLINE

www.ingramcontent.com/pod-product-compliance
Lightning Source LLC
Chambersburg PA
CBHW081242180526
45171CB00005B/513